THE POETRY WITCH
LITTLE BOOK
OF
GODDESS POEMS

THE POETRY WITCH LITTLE BOOK OF GODDESS POEMS

BY ANNIE FINCH

POETRY WITCH PRESS

Poetry Witch Press
Brooklyn, NY, USA
www.anniefinch.com

© 2025 Poetry Witch Press
All rights reserved

Book design by Sophia Renda

9781737307587

For the Goddesses

CONTENTS

Baubo's Dance 10

Brigid 11

Changing Woman 12

Coatlicue 13

Demeter in Her Garden 14

Eve 16

Her Forest 17

The Gravity of Goddess 18

At the Trivial Crossing of Hekate 19

Inanna 20

To the Priestess of Inanna After 4500 Years 21

Kali 22

To the Goddesses of Fortune 23

The Hail Mother 24

Chain of Women 25

The Priestesses are Singing Slow 26

In Sekhmet's New Temple 27

Spider Woman 28

Goddess Riding the Sun 29

BAUBO'S DANCE

Between my legs there is a mind
Before before and after after.

Join me here and you will find
Root and roar and wild laughter.

Join me here and we'll learn blind.
Faster. Slower. Slower. Faster.

Faster. Slower. Slower. Faster.
Long before and after after,

Join me here and you will find
Root and roar and wild laughter.

Join me here in the unwinding —
Faster. Slower. Slower. Faster.

Spin with me — and Spin with me —
and Spin with me and you will find

Between my legs there is a mind
Before before and after after.

BRIGID

Ring, ring, ring, ring! Hammers fall.
Your gold will all be beaten
over sudden flaming fire
moving from you, the pyre. Sweeten
your cauldron, until the sun
runs with one flame through the day
and the healing water will sing,
linger on tongues, burn away.

CHANGING WOMAN

If we change as she is changing,
if she changes as we change

(If she changes, I am changing)

Who is changing, as I bend
down to what the sky has sent us?

(Is she changing, or the same?)

COATLICUE

She listens for breathing
around her in the night.
Below the mountain,
families are sleeping.
When will she wake
to bring the morning?
When will she birth

sun and stars?
When will her mist
give birth to the moon?

The skulls are breathing,
as quiet in her necklace
as darkness will keep them.

DEMETER IN HER GARDEN

Demeter found me, or rather, I found her
when her tomatoes were nodding and green
under the shelter of the side of her barn
near an acre of fields, wild with an orchard,
the long grass pushing up under the trees,
and hyssop, bee balm, lavender, chicory,
mallow, johnny jump up, love in a mist,
coneflower, blackeyed susan, lavender, broccoli,
in her circular garden that curved from the earth.

When we walked up, she was crouched in that circle,
picking peas from a strong tangled vine.
I waited and watched, while her mountainous body
filled my vision until I was quiet,
and the arms of the planet held me alive.
Her hands were as wide, cool, and earth-stained
as mossy old rocks that a forest has patiently
grown up around, died around, fallen near.
and pulls through the earth. Then my body was hers,
spine in the planet, blood in the wind,
as she dropped the peas in the aluminum bowl.

Idly, I'd been pulling deeply
at some weeds growing down in the herbs.
I felt very tired, and very afraid,
and, suddenly, filled with the earth's oldest memories.

I'd been invaded; the baby was not mine.
Why should I carry it? Coneflowers blew
fuschia and silent, as if there was laughter,
from the breeze that was suddenly simpler,
as if there could once more be joy. It had been
months since I'd felt like myself at all,
months since my life had moved for me.

I didn't say anything, watching her shoulders
as she finished picking, and raised herself, squinting
at the sun stretching down on the garden.
"When my daughter Persephone was young," she said finally,
"she cried every time I pulled weeds. It was hard
to see that. It's hard to let go, but we need to."

We went inside quietly, washed off our hands,
and that night I slept in the bed in her barn,
where dreams of the animals nuzzled and licked me
through my long dreams. I woke up with a road,
a path, and a promise...
I walked to the bus station, feet moving quietly
on the earth, the cement, and the asphalt,
eyes moving calm over trees, streetlights, buildings.

.

EVE

When mother Eve took the first apple down
from the tree that grew where nature's heart had been
and came tumbling, circling, rosy, into sin,
which goddesses were lost, and which were found?
What spirals moved in pity and unwound
across our mother's body with the spin
of planets lost for us and all her kin?
What serpents curved their mouths into a frown,
but left their bodies twined in us like threads
that lead us back to her? Her presence warms,
and if I follow closely through the maze,
it is to where her remembered reaching spreads
in branching gifts, it is to her reaching arms
that I reach, as if for something near to praise.

HER FOREST

Her forest goes as green as love.
Her ferns are dappled near the ground,
and moss they dappled curls above
stones that Her glacier dappled down.

Her night is sadness well-contained
within the sap that runs the stem
of plants that grow along the night
and root at morning. Joy finds them,

and oceans, lost because they are vast
(like ruined roads left on the land)
take Her kind waters home each time
that they, pushing raptly at the sand,

make tides with Her evaporate rain.
The ocean is at peace again.
Far algae grows, the blue stays smooth,
And in dim light, the beach is soothed.

Her forest goes as green as love,
Her night is sadness well-contained,
and oceans, lost because they are vast,
make tides with Her evaporate rain.

THE GRAVITY OF GODDESS

The gravity of goddess is above
My eyes, when I look up like someone's child.
There is no spoken sentence. All she says
will stay. It will be quiet when I go
out of the room and stop being a priestess.
She looks down. Her quiet death is unashamed,
undimming power like receding grain
that waves inside my heart in shocking rag-
ing silence, beating in the window light.
She will not go to make new presences,
but stays to go. Her presence is the loss.

In the cold sky that waits each season out,
her body's ancient stars make restless calls
against the throne that quivers in my heart
as fiercely in love as in the hate
on which four thousand years of sorrow fed.

Her birdsong joys shine ruins in my heart.
I seem to stand on some undying plain,
watching the monuments that dawn again.
The gravity of goddess is above
my eyes, though never gone from history.
So many must have noticed, with this shock,
such patient looking up, and looking down.

AT THE TRIVIAL CROSSING OF HEKATE

As the moon turned dark, we have stopped and sung
To the maiden and the mother, where the months are hung.

By our seeds! By our months! by our days!
Triple goddesses, we cried, amazed!

Where three roads meet, we have stood and cried
Till the hands of the Goddesses beckoned us inside.

By our seeds! By our months! by our days!
Triple goddesses, we turn, amazed!

She's alive in the crossroads that center the Earth!
She is pooling the centuries' still, dry, hard salt!

By our seeds! By our months! by our days!
Triple goddesses, we burn, amazed!

She's the Queen of the Darkness, who touches our fault
Into flame! We can birth through her — trivial — Birth!

By our seeds! By our months! by our days!
Triple goddesses, we learn, amazed!

INANNA

A young goddess, full of love,
fresh with the touch of a husband,
carrying power and rich with anger,
strength, urgency, understanding,
follows the direction her ear has led her,
down to the place where the underworld glistens.

At each door she removes a jewel,
a belt, a ceremonial robe.
At each door, she is less and more.
She bows down through the seventh door.

The young goddess is dead, and waiting.
The young goddess is dead.
A goddess goes down, and I can see her.
She needs to go, decides to go.
A goddess goes down, and I can hear her.

TO THE PRIESTESS OF INANNA AFTER 4500 YEARS

> *"I no longer dwell in the goodly place you established ...*
> *My honey-sweet voice has become strident."*
> — Enheduanna, Priestess of Inanna in Sumer,
> The Descent of Inanna *(23rd Century BC;*
> *trans. Kramer and Wolkstein)*

Star-tongued chanter, o priestess in voice and in state,
Stone-haired Mother of poets who named yourself proudly,
You of *honey-sweet voice* and of *most bitter fate* —

Once you blazed down your Goddess through the seventh cold gate
Till she crawled through the Underworld on naked knee!
Star-tongued chanter, o priestess in voice and in state,

Then you killed her. You stripped off her ornaments' weight
And she hung on the hook of revenge and cruelty.
You of *honey-sweet voice* and of *most bitter fate,*

For three days, for three nights, as the stars wheeled and ate,
Her *contentiousness and disobedience* shook like a key.
Star-tongued chanter, o priestess in voice and in state,

Then — you saved her! Blaze, now! Burn us home to your great
Queen of Roses, Inanna — as strong as she's free!
You of *honey-sweet voice* and of *most bitter fate,*

Sing us home to when it was not almost too late!
Sing us home where Goddesses are ready to be!
Star-tongued chanter, o, priestess, in voice — and in state! —
Free your *honey-sweet song! Sing us back our sweet fate!*

KALI

I walked cautiously, knowing my belly
full of wide wings, night, and starlight.

The dark highway led me from the others,
and then a narrow path led to Kali.
I could see her, sitting, sewing
on a huge tapestry as rich as blood.

I walked cautiously, knowing my belly
full of wide wings, night, and starlight.

I saw in its folds a glimpse of creation,
animals, planets, mountains, and trees,
embroidered thick with contrasts and colors,
on a background as warm as blood.

I walked cautiously, knowing my belly
full of wide wings, night, and starlight.

Did I have to explain what I wanted?
Did she wait till I tried to explain?

No, of course not; she'd known my story
before I had come. She was Kali.

I walked cautiously, knowing my belly
full of wide wings, night, and starlight.

TO THE GODDESSES OF FORTUNE

Moneta, Asase Ya, Aja, Lakshmi, Eopsin, Fortuna . . .

You have washed me like a potion
In the rains that have no shore;
You've diluted, drenched, and faded,
Drowned me, carried me no more,
Goddesses of every fortune,
Small and close, and far like doom.

You have buried, rusted, rotted
All I needed, like a tomb;
you have moved me like a dancer,
Taught me, freed me — made me room,
Goddesses of every fortune,
Small and close, and far like doom.

You have turned me like a chalice
In the wind that hollows home
Till the grains of sand have pitted
My humilities to air,
Goddesses of every fortune,
Small and close, and far like doom.

You have forged me like a cauldron
In the flame that marries forms.
You have burned me, melted, fused me,
Bent and charred me, left me cold,
Goddesses of every fortune,
Small and close, and far like doom;
You have moved me like a dancer,
Taught me, freed me — made me room.

THE HAIL MOTHER

Hail Mother, full of power,
Your children are with thee.
Blessed are you and all the Goddesses,
and blessed is the fruit of your womb: me.
Holy Mother, Mother of all,
I give you joy and gratitude —
Now and at the hour of my death.

CHAIN OF WOMEN

These are the seasons Persephone promised
as she turned on her heel —
the ones that darken, till green no longer
bandages what I feel.

Now touches of gold stipple the branches,
promising weeks of time
to fade through, finding the footprints
she left as she turned to climb.

THE PRIESTESSES ARE SINGING SLOW

Heavy curtains close around our golden
Powers. We will wake in the dark noon
And seed quick shadows over the white embers;
We touch the pages; patterns cascade down.
And the folds of our robes fall like water,
Floating candles swell with secret grain,
And the long-hovering words begin to rain.
Even a book is simple in our folded
World. Though Her throne is hidden, the horn-shaped moon
Glows where our feet have touched Her. We remember
Pillars opening to petals (they are our own).
Such a quiet birth holds us. Earth's old daughters,
We keep our wisdom. We carry our own crowns.

IN SEKHMET'S NEW TEMPLE

You've guided me, Sekhmet — there's no turning back —
The desert is blooming — and so is my heart —
its — ripe inner — channels — are blossoming black

with their lioness beauty till there is no lack.
The moon on your temple floor loves — me — apart—
You're guiding me, Sekhmet — there's no turning back

The push of — your will — at the small of my back —
That guides me — now — Sekhmet — (there's no turning — back —
Your fierce eyes are open!) — Your peace will enact

its all-needing flames, unrelenting, to track,
to turn me — to toss me — until our Will — starts —
You've guided me, Sekhmet. There's no turning back

the touch of — your voice — in this close — sudden crack —
The desert is blooming — and so is my heart —
The matrix — home — center, Your temple, is — back —

SPIDER WOMAN

Your thoughts in a web have covered the sky.
A thread from the northwest is carrying beads from the rain,
a thread from the southwest is carrying beads from the rain,
a thread from the southeast carries bright beads,
a thread from the northeast is bringing the beads
of the rain that has filled up the sky.
Spider, you have woven a chain
stretching with rain over the sky.

GODDESS RIDING THE SUN

For Adrienne Rich

As a Mother — like flame — takes life back,
We are changed! Flame is all that She has,
Rising up from the coals to the sky;
She is here! Where She glows on the same,

We are changed! Flame is all that She has,
Since she gave up her land once. We call;
She is here! And She glows on the same,
Rising up from the coals, to the sky,

Since she gave up her land, once. We call
Past the embers She's leaving to stay,
Rising down from the roots, to the sky,
Breathing green-yellow peace through the night.

Past the embers, She's leaving to stay,
To return as a creature again —
Breathing green-yellow peace through the night
As we lie with our softer new hearts.

She returns, as a creature again —
She is riding the Sun like a crown
As we lie with our softer new hearts
Where Her body remembers the trees.

Goddess Riding the Sun! Come to be
As a Mother — like flame! Take us back
Where Your body remembers the trees
Rising down from the roots to the sky!

ACKNOWLEDGEMENTS

"Aphrodite," first collected in *Eve* (Story Line Press, 1997, Reprinted by Carnegie Mellon University Press Contemporary Classics Poetry Series, 2011)

"Brigid," first collected in *Eve* (Story Line Press, 1997, Reprinted by Carnegie Mellon University Press Contemporary Classics Poetry Series, 2011)

"Changing Woman," first collected in *Eve* (Story Line Press, 1997, Reprinted by Carnegie Mellon University Press Contemporary Classics Poetry Series, 2011)

"Coatlicue," first collected in *Eve* (Story Line Press, 1997, Reprinted by Carnegie Mellon University Press Contemporary Classics Poetry Series, 2011)

"Demeter in Her Garden," excerpted from *Among the Goddesses: An Epic Libretto in Seven Dreams* (Red Hen Press, 2010)

"Eve," first collected in *Eve* (Story Line Press, 1997, Reprinted by Carnegie Mellon University Press Contemporary Classics Poetry Series, 2011)

"Your Forest," first published in *National Poetry Review*

"The Gravity of Goddess," first collected in *Spells: New and Selected Poems* (Wesleyan University Press, 2013)

"Inanna," first collected in *Eve* (Story Line Press, 1997, Reprinted by Carnegie Mellon University Press Contemporary Classics Poetry Series, 2011)

"Kali," excerpted and adapted from *Among the Goddesses: An Epic Libretto in Seven Dreams* (Red Hen Press, 2010)

"Chain of Women," first collected in *Calendars* (Tupelo Press, 2003, second edition with CD, 2008)

"The Priestesses Are Singing Slow," published in *Image*

"In Sekhmet's New Temple," first appeared in *MaternalGiftEconomy.com*

"Spider Woman," first collected in *Eve* (Story Line Press, 1997, Reprinted by Carnegie Mellon University Press Contemporary Classics Poetry Series, 2011)

"Goddess Riding the Sun," first published in *Pensive*

ABOUT THE POET

Annie Finch is the author of seven volumes of poetry, including *Calendars* and *Eve*, both finalists for the National Poetry Series, and *Spells: New and Selected Poems* (Wesleyan University Press). Her poetry has been featured in periodicals such as the *New York Times, Poetry Magazine,* and *The Paris Review* and books such as *The Penguin Book of Twentieth-Century American Poetry, Penguin Book of the Sonnet,* and *Norton Anthology of World Literature*. Finch is also the author of *A Poet's Craft: A Comprehensive Guide to Making and Sharing Your Poetry* and editor of ten anthologies including *A Formal Feeling Comes,Villanelles, An Exaltation of Forms, Measure for Measure: An Anthology of Poetic Meters*, and *Choice Words: Writers on Abortion*. Her other works include prosody, essays on poetics, poetry translation, and collaborations with choral music, opera, theater, and dance. Finch's work has been a finalist for the Yale Series of Younger Poets and Foreword Book Award and honored with the Arlt Prize, Sarasvati Award, and Robert Fitzgerald Award. She earned a Ph.D from Stanford University and served for a decade as Director of the Stonecoast MFA Program in Creative Writing. She is based in New York City and offers workshops and performances worldwide. For more information, please visit anniefinch.com